EXPLORING SPACE

CONTENTS

Translated from the Italian and edited
by Maureen Spurgeon

Text by Stefano Sibella
Illustrated by Davide Bonadonna

Left: three stages of the formation of a star. Below: what the Big Bang probably looked like.

Beyond the Earth

There are more stars in the Universe than there are grains of sands on all the beaches in the world. The Universe is so vast that a ray of light travelling from a remote part of Outer Space takes millions of years to reach the Earth. So, when astronomers observe the most distant galaxies, they see them as they were when they were formed, millions and millions of years ago – only one billion years after the birth of the Universe itself. Radio-telescopes are used to study these galaxies, and the further away they are, the further back we look in time.

The constellation of Pleiades (the 'Seven Sisters')

The origin of the Universe

15 billion years ago and within the tiniest length of time – something like a millionth of a billionth of a billionth of a second, there was an explosion in Space. This explosion is known as the **Big Bang**. This was when the Universe began, instantly expanding at a temperature of billions of billions of billions of degrees and rapidly becoming billions and billions and billions times more vast.

Most scientists believe in the theory of the Big Bang, but there are some who talk of **'cosmic strings'** (long strands of mass energy), of **'parallel dimensions'**, and of a never-ending **expansion-contraction**. In the future, we may know more...

ENORMOUS MEASUREMENTS

Our Sun is only one star among an estimated 200 billion stars which orbit in a galaxy called the Milky Way. The Earth is also part of this galaxy. The Milky Way is like an enormous belt in Space with branches and spirals 60,000 light years away. (One light year equals about 9.5 million, million kilometres – the distance which light travels in one year.) The Milky Way is only one of about 50 billion galaxies in the Universe and these galaxies are part of huge masses of galaxies. The largest known mass of galaxies in the Universe extends 650 million light years into Outer Space.

FACT

Space is so vast that the most powerful space rocket would take at least 100,000 years to reach the star nearest the Sun!

Far Away and 'Near'

Venus is the nearest planet to Earth. **Andromeda** is the nearest galaxy. Both are visible to the naked eye (without a telescope or binoculars). At least another 3000 heavenly bodies can be seen from the Earth on a clear night, from a distance of 40 million kilometres to 2.8 million light years. The **Moon** is the nearest heavenly body to our planet, and **Proxima Centauri,** part of the constellation **Centaurus,** is the nearest star – 'only' 4.3 light years away.

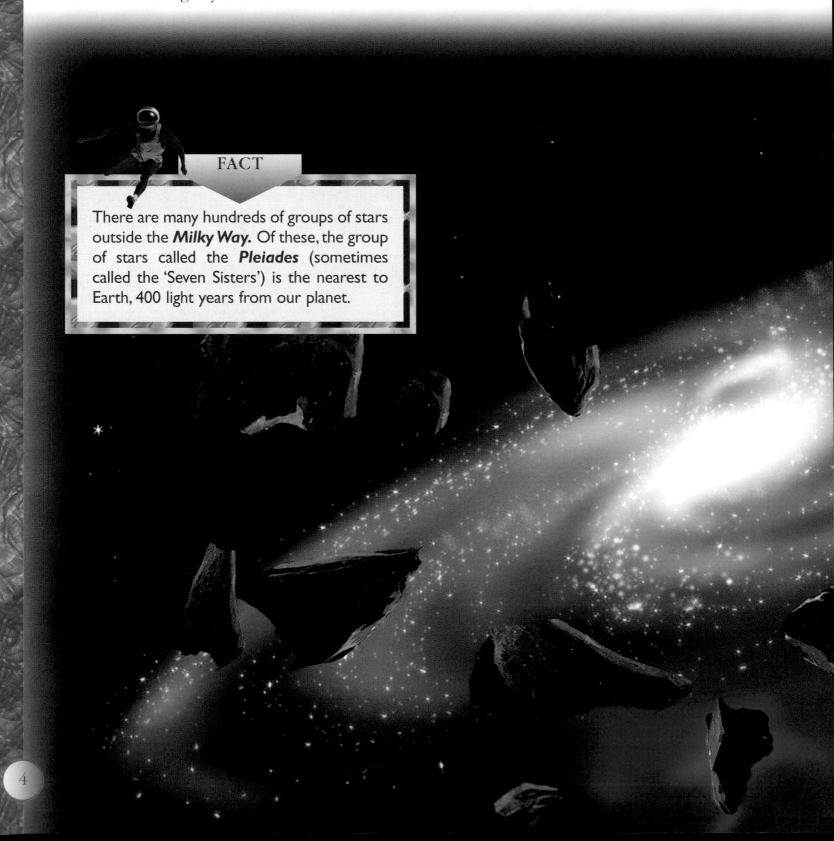

FACT

There are many hundreds of groups of stars outside the **Milky Way.** Of these, the group of stars called the **Pleiades** (sometimes called the 'Seven Sisters') is the nearest to Earth, 400 light years from our planet.

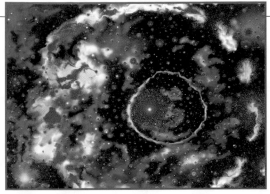

Above: the centre of the Milky Way, surrounded by a ring of cosmic gas.

Below: our galaxy, the Milky Way.

THE CONSTELLATIONS

*A constellation is a group of stars with a particular shape or pattern. There are 88 **constellations** in the part of the sky which we can see from Earth. The largest of these constellations is **Hydra,** which covers a surface equal to 3.16% of the whole sky and has at least 68 stars. The smallest of these is the **Southern Cross** which takes up a 'space' equal to 0.16% of the entire sky.*

Giant Stars, Shooting Stars

The famous Halley's Comet

Stars can be medium-sized, such as our **Sun,** but there are also 'giants' and 'dwarfs'. To get some idea of size – if our Sun were as large as a football, a 'giant' star would be as big as a ball large enough to contain a small city, and a 'dwarf' star would be the size of a billiard ball. **Betelgeuse** is a 'super-giant' star with a diameter 750 times larger than that of our Sun.

Betelgeuse is part of the constellation **Orion. Antares** in the **Scorpius** constellation is another 'super-giant', 640 times larger than the Sun.

Even more distant are stars with old, mythical names – **Mira, (Cetus constellation), Deneb, (Cygnus), Aldebaran (Taurus)** and **Canopus,** (also known as Alpha Carinas) a star

FACT

The largest **comet** ever seen passed near the Sun in 1843. Its tail was over 330 million kilometres long and it went from the Sun on to Mars.

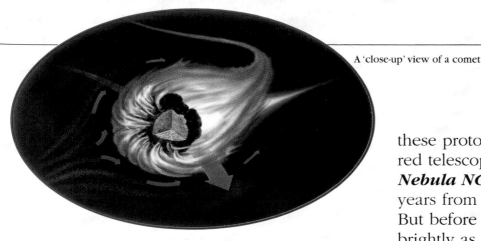

A 'close-up' view of a comet

these protostars can only be detected by infra-red telescopes. These protostars are in the **Nebula NGC 1333,** at a distance of 1100 light years from Earth.

But before these protostars can sparkle as brightly as Sirius, at least another 100,000 years must pass.

The oldest stars in the Milky Way – about seventy of them – are at the top of the disc of the galaxy, formed about a billion years after the **Big Bang,** around 14 billion years ago.

in the **Carina Constellation** and second only to **Sirius** (the 'dog star') for brightness. The 'youngest' stars in the **Milky Way** are two protostars called **IRAS-4. IRAS** stands for **Infra-Red Astronomy Satellite**, because

Stars with a tail

Comets are found at the very edges of the Solar System, where it is colder than we could ever imagine. A comet has the appearance of a great big 'dirty snowball'. The larger comets take thousands of years to complete their orbit around the Sun – for instance, **Encke's Comet** takes 3302 years and **Pons-Winnecke's Comet**, 6125 years. Other comets return close to the Sun at intervals of centuries or decades.

Faster than Light

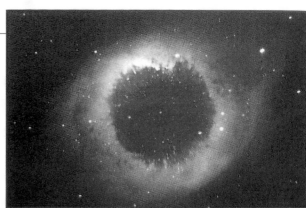
The Helix nebula

In the Universe, a beam of light travels faster than anything else. The **Sun,** the **Earth** and the whole **Solar System** orbit around at the centre of the Milky Way, at an incredible speed of 900,000 kilometres per hour. Yet, in just one second, light travels at least 300,000 kilometres. In one hour, it can cover a distance equal to 1078 million kilometres. In one year, light travels about 9.5 million, million kilometres – a distance which astronomers usually define as one *light year.* So, the time taken for light to travel from **Earth** to the **Moon** is about 1.3 seconds, to reach Pluto, six hours, and, to go on to the edges of our galaxy, the **Milky Way,** 100,000 years. For light from the Earth to land within **Andromeda,** our nearest galaxy, would take 2.8 million years. To reach the limits of the Universe light would take 15 billion years, to the time when we believe the Universe began.

The brightest heavenly bodies

The brightest star in the sky is **Sirius** which the ancient Greeks knew as 'the shining one'. Sirius is part of the constellation **Canis Major** and is about twice as large and 20 times brighter than our Sun. But the heavenly body which is the brightest in the whole of Space is *quasar HS 1946+7658* – which is 15 times brighter than the Sun. (A quasar is the nucleus of a very old galaxy which sends out radio waves and travels at a speed close to the speed of light.) At the other end of the scale, the darkest heavenly bodies, the *obscure nebulae,* can just about be seen.

FACT

An expert driver at the wheel of a racing car travelling at top speed would need an endless supply of fuel and would take 340 billion years – 25 times more than the age of the Universe – to reach the 'finishing line' at the centre of the Milky Way.

WHERE TEETH WOULD CHATTER...

A nebula is a cloud of dust and gas in space. The **Boomerang nebula,** *so-called because the nebula is boomerang-shaped, is 5000 light years distant from the Earth and one of the coldest places in the Universe, where a temperature of -426°C has been recorded. But even this is mild, compared to the temperature of* **Triton,** *one of the moons of Neptune, with an average temperature of -495°C by day.*

Observing the Universe

The Hubble Deep Field shows the most distant images in space

To observe Space, astronomers use highly sophisticated optical instruments, such as **telescopes.** Simple binoculars today have approximately the same power to observe the night sky as **Galileo's telescope,** invented in 1610. The most highly-developed telescope in use today is the **Hubble Space Telescope** which orbits at the highest level of the atmosphere and transmits to Earth the clearest images of heavenly bodies ever seen. The Hubble Space Telescope is about the same size as a bus and it completes an entire orbit around the Earth every 90 minutes. **Chandra,** the most powerful X-ray telescope in the world, has an orbit which is 200 times more far-reaching than the Hubble Space Telescope. Imagine a car-driver being able to identify and read an ordinary street map at a distance of 20 kilometres and you get some idea of Chandra's power in receiving images in Space.

Left, Galileo's telescope.

Below, the *Hubble Space Telescope*

The Arecibo radio-telescope

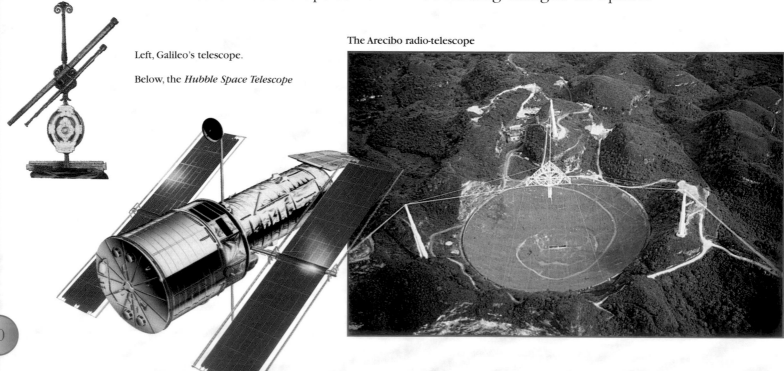

ever seen with a telescope – including heavenly bodies in formation.

The two **Keck telescopes** at the **Mauna Kea Observatory** in Hawaii are the largest optical telescopes in the world, with mirrors 10 metres in diameter within their enormous, huge domes.

The **Very Large Array** in New Mexico (US) is the most modern and one of the largest radio-telescopes in use. Its 27 enormous antennae capture each radio signal transmitted from planets, stars, galaxies and space vehicles.

In 1974, astronomers sent signals from the radio-telescope **Arecibo** to **M13,** a star cluster so distant that, should space aliens eventually receive the message, their answer would not reach Earth until about the year 44,000.

After the year 2007, the **Next Generation Space Telescope** will be launched into lunar orbit. This will use a mirror 8 metres in diameter which will have different sections. Each section will be able to open and turn out towards Space like the petals of a flower. Then we shall see more beautiful things!

The six telescopes of the *Darwin Space Project.* In the near future these will enable important discoveries to be made outside the Solar System.

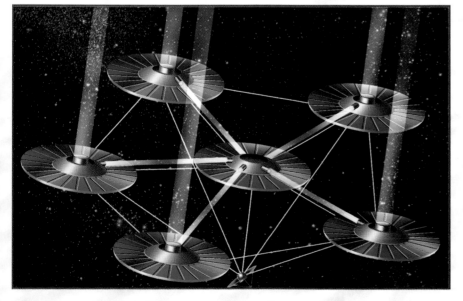

Prototype of the
Next Generation Telescope.

The Solar System

The **Solar System** (illustrated on the right), is made up of the **Sun** and a large number of heavenly bodies which orbit (travel around) it. These heavenly bodies include 9 **planets,** 61 **moons, asteroids, comets** and a huge quantity of **dust** and **gas,** which is all that remains of **cosmic clouds** that originated about 5 billion years ago.

THE SUN

The **Sun** *is a star, like billions of other stars in the galaxy. Although it is only a small star, it constitutes about 99.99% of the entire Solar System and could contain the Earth about 1,400,000 times! The Sun is composed mainly of hydrogen and helium. The nuclear pressure within the Sun is up to 2000 billion times more than that registered on the Earth's surface. Its temperature hovers around 14 million degrees Centigrade. The external layer of the Sun, the* **photosphere,** *has a thickness of around 300 kilometres and reaches a heat of 5000°C.*

From the first appearance of the dinosaurs, over 200 million years ago, the Sun has completed just one entire orbit around the Milky Way...

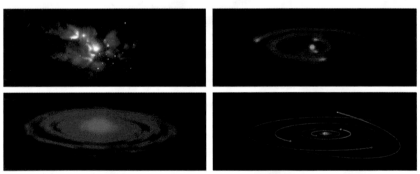

The different phases of formation of the planets.

FACT

In one second, the **Sun** generates more energy than that which has been consumed by the human race in the course of its entire history. A powerful cross-country vehicle, launched into Space at top speed would take 170 years to go from the Earth to the Sun.

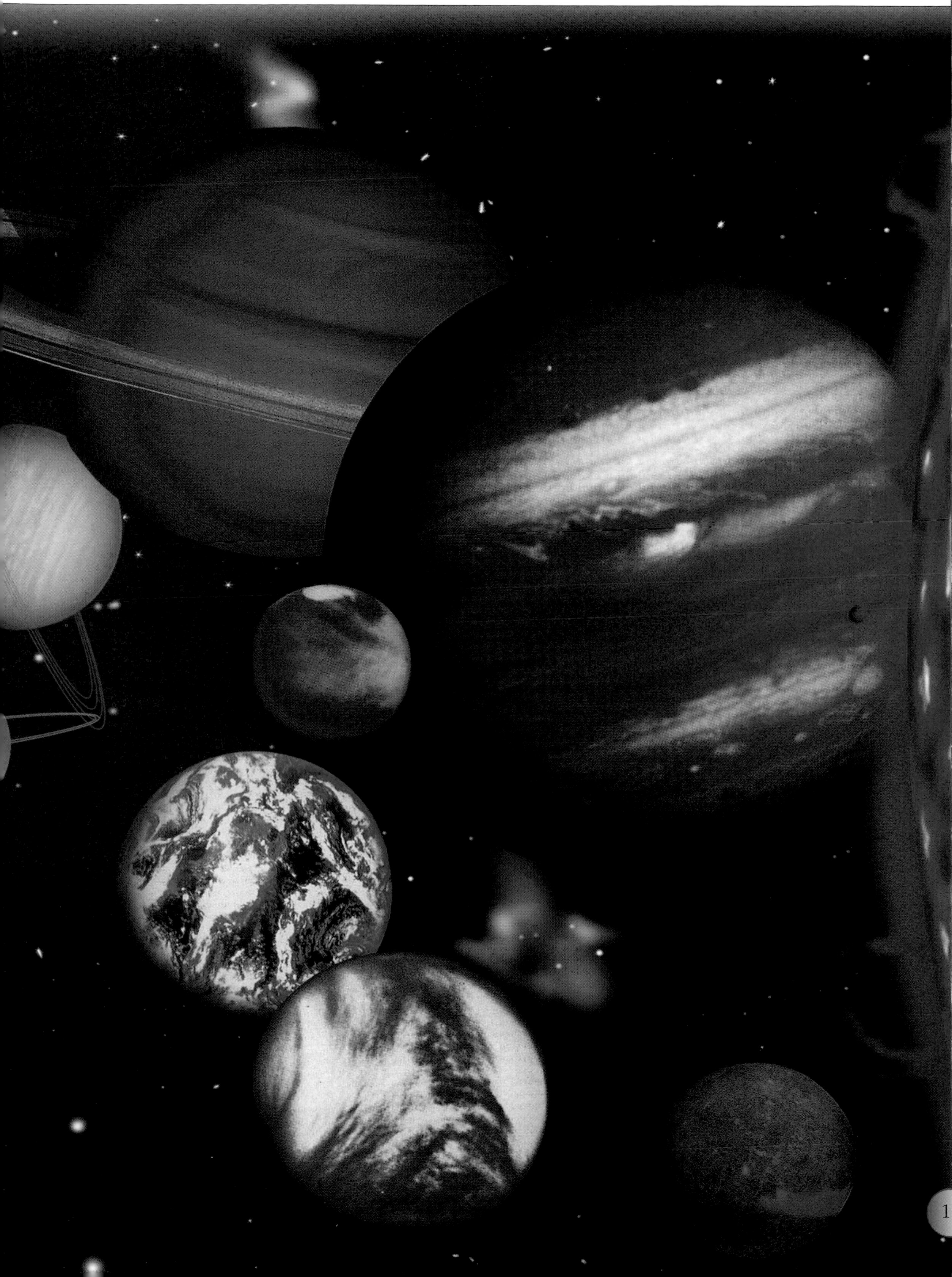

Asteroids

Orbiting around the **Sun** and between the planets **Mars** and **Jupiter,** there are thousands of rocky masses (about 4000 of which we know about). These rocky masses are called **asteroids** – some so distant from each other, that if we could travel on a spacecraft into the region of space where asteroids are most numerous, we might not even see one.
Ceres, the largest asteroid, has a diameter of 1000 kilometres. But there are others with diameters of 100 kilometres. The smallest asteroid known so far, **1993 KA2,** has a diameter of barely 5 metres. If all the asteroids in the Solar System were put together, their combined size would be less than a third of the Moon.

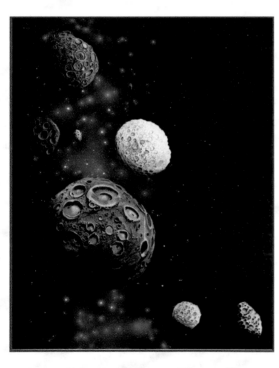

Asteroids never travel alone through space. Instead, they group together in great masses, something like that depicted in the illustration on the left. Below, a rocky object from the 'asteroid belt' in Space. To the right, a meteorite as it crashes into another object in space.

FACT

The largest **meteorite** (fragment of an asteroid falling to Earth) was found in Africa, in Namibia. It was 2.7 metres long by 2.4 metres wide and weighed over 60 tonnes... as heavy as 11 elephants!

GIANT STONES, FALLING STARS

A whole multitude of small rocks, fragments of comets, orbit around the **Sun.** *These rocky fragments are called meteors. Each day some collide with other heavenly bodies, or fall to Earth, when they are defined as* **meteorites.** *It is estimated that only about once in tens of millions of years would a meteorite be large enough to cause a disaster. More often, a meteorite is only as big as a stone. The largest crater made by a meteorite is the* **Meteor Crater** *in Arizona, USA. This crater measures more than 1200 metres in diameter, 183 metres deep, and is believed to have been made about 50,000 years ago.*

Mercury

Mercury is the planet nearest the Sun. By day, within the craters on its surface, the temperature averages between 350-400°C. But by night, this drops to at least -170°C due to the lack of atmosphere. Mercury's nucleus of iron and nickel is larger than the Moon. The *Caloris Basin,* one of Mercury's craters, is half as large as the whole of North America.

Mercury orbits around the Sun on a very stretched-out, elongated orbit at a much faster speed than any other planet. It has a diameter of 4878 kilometres and one day on Mercury lasts the equivalent to 58.6 days on Earth – which means that Mercury has a year equal to 88 Earth days. The average distance from Mercury to the Sun is 58 million kilometres.

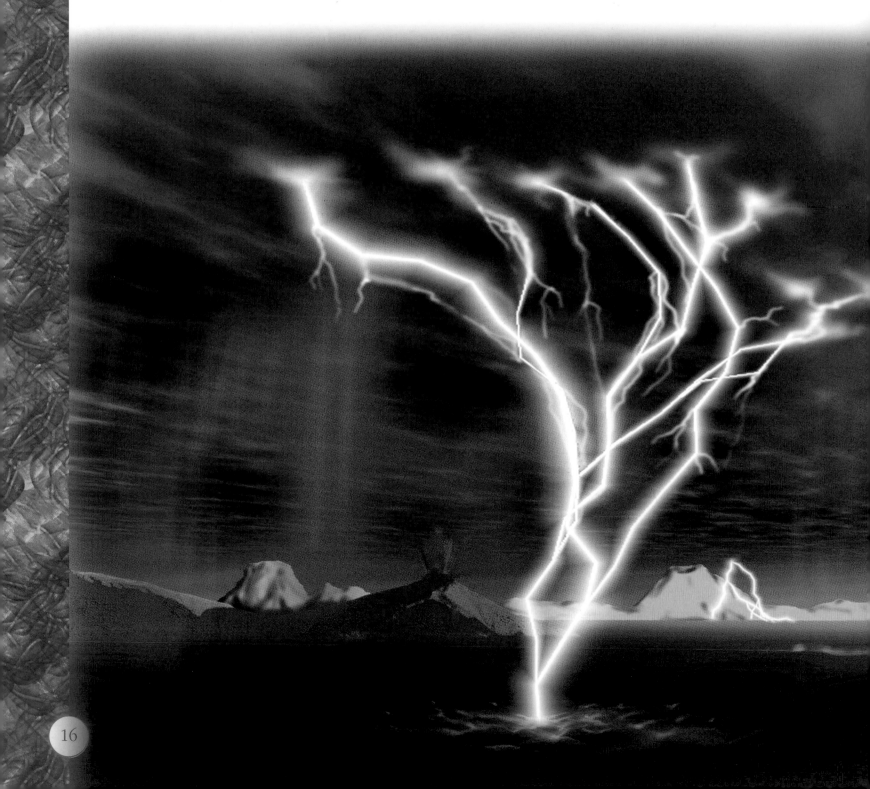

Venus

After the Sun and the Moon, the planet **Venus** is the brightest heavenly body seen from the Earth. It is also the hottest and most inhospitable planet in the entire Solar System. Surrounded by a thick blanket of cloud, and with a dense atmosphere of carbon dioxide, its vast plain with 167 extremely high volcanoes on the surface, some over 8000 metres high, the ground temperature of Venus is at least 480°C – hot enough to melt even lead. It is constantly battered by sulphuric acid rain and the pressure of the air is at least 90 times that of the Earth. The diameter of Venus is 12,104 kilometres, and one Venus day equals 243 days on Earth. One year on Venus lasts as long as 225 Earth years. The average distance from Venus to the Sun is 108 million kilometres.

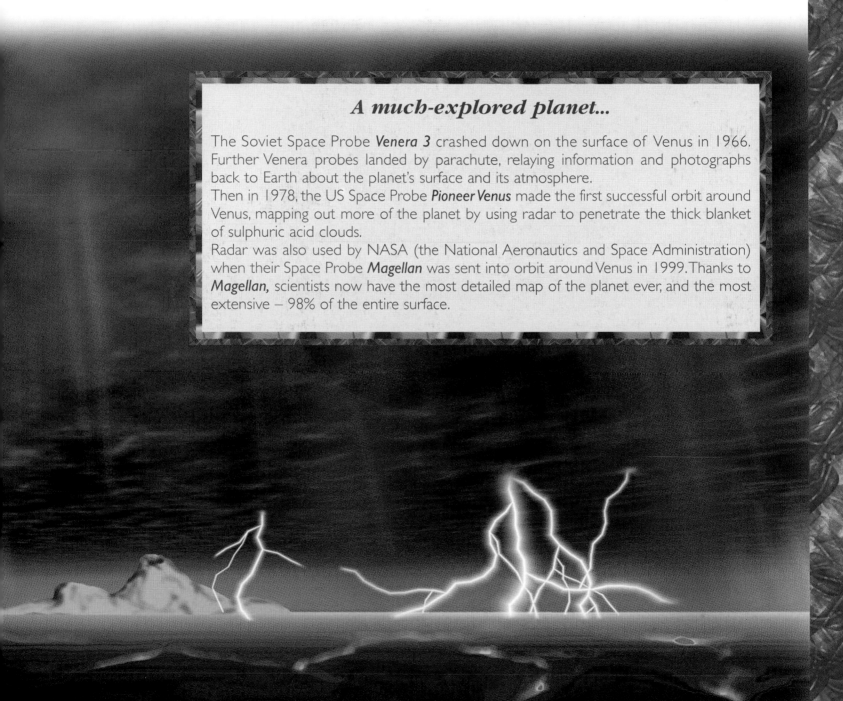

A much-explored planet...

The Soviet Space Probe **Venera 3** crashed down on the surface of Venus in 1966. Further Venera probes landed by parachute, relaying information and photographs back to Earth about the planet's surface and its atmosphere.

Then in 1978, the US Space Probe **Pioneer Venus** made the first successful orbit around Venus, mapping out more of the planet by using radar to penetrate the thick blanket of sulphuric acid clouds.

Radar was also used by NASA (the National Aeronautics and Space Administration) when their Space Probe **Magellan** was sent into orbit around Venus in 1999. Thanks to **Magellan,** scientists now have the most detailed map of the planet ever, and the most extensive – 98% of the entire surface.

Earth

The diameter of the **Earth** is 12,756 kilometres. One day lasts 24 hours, there are 365.26 days in each year, and the average distance from the Sun is 149.6 kilometres. Earth has an internal nucleus of solid iron, very, very hot and with a thickness of 1000 kilometres. Its external nucleus is liquid iron, 2400 kilometres thick.

The external nucleus is surrounded by a rocky 'mantle' 2800 kilometres down into the depths of the planet and then a surface crust, rather like the skin of a fruit. Earth's crust is 35 kilometres thick beneath the continents and 5-10 kilometres thick beneath the oceans.

FACT

In its orbit around the Sun, Earth travels at a speed of 30 kilometres per second – 1800 kilometres per minute – at the same time spinning on its own axis at 1700 kilometres per hour. The drilling at a platinum mine at **Zapolyarny** in Russia holds the record for excavation, digging down to a depth of 15 kilometres – just a 'scratch' on the crust of the Earth. Digging at a rate of 10 centimetres each minute, it would take a good 261 years to dig a tunnel through the Earth – if such a feat were possible!

THE MOON

*The diameter of the **Moon** is about one quarter that of the Earth (3476 kilometres). The average distance from Earth is 384,000 kilometres. The surface of the Moon covers the same area as the continent of Africa, with a temperature which varies between -155°C and -105°C. The force of gravity is equal to one sixth of that on Earth – so, on the Moon, a person weighs six times less than on Earth, which means a human being can jump higher than a kangaroo, making footprints which last millions of years... On the surface of the Moon, it does not rain and the wind does not blow! Moon is Earth's satellite, and so far, it is the only heavenly body on which humans have landed.*

Mars

Mars is the fourth planet from the Sun at a distance of 228 million kilometres. It leans at an angle in its orbit, in a similar way to Earth. Mars also has ice-caps and seasons similar to that of our 'blue planet' and a temperature at its Equator which in summer can reach 20°C. More often the climate remains stable below zero, falling to -80°C by night.

Olympus Mons is an ancient volcano on Mars, now extinct. It is the highest mountain in the whole Solar System, three times higher than Mount Everest. The **Valles Marineris** is a canyon which is so long that the Grand Canyon in Arizona seems like a small scratch. One day on the 'red planet' lasts 24.6 Earth hours, one year 687 Earth days, and its diameter is 6794 kilometres.

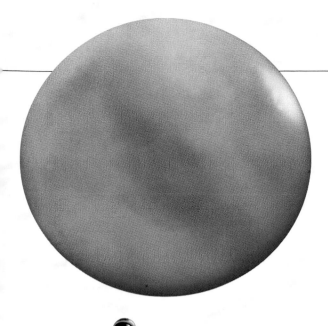

THE MOONS OF MARS

Around **Mars** *there orbits two small moons shaped rather like giant potatoes –* **Phobos** *at 28 kilometres diameter and* **Deimos** *with a diameter of 16 kilometres, the smallest satellite in the Solar System and 40 million times smaller than our Moon. The force of gravity on Deimos is so weak that if any future space travellers were to jump on its surface, they would find themselves flying off into Space.*

FACT

If the ice on **Mars** were to melt, its surface would be flooded by an ocean with depths of between 10 and 100 metres.

Europa

Jupiter

Jupiter is the largest planet in the Solar System – so large that our Earth could fit inside it more than 1000 times! The planet is covered by a thick layer of cloud and strong winds whirl around a sphere made up of a small rocky nucleus and a thick mantle of gas. Jupiter's diameter is 142,800 kilometres, one day lasts 9.8 Earth hours, and one year equals 11.8 Earth years. The average distance from the Sun is 778 million kilometres.

FACT

The **Great Red Spot** is an enormous cyclone which shakes the whole planet at least once every 300 years. Compared to its power and strength, the most devastating hurricane on Earth would only be a puff of wind....

The Moons of Jupiter

Jupiter boasts at least 16 moons. The largest four, *Ganymede, Callisto, Io* and *Europa* were discovered in 1610 by Galileo Galilei. *Ganymede* is the largest satellite in the entire Solar System, 2017 larger than our Moon, and even as large as planets such as Mercury and Pluto. *Io* is entirely covered by volcanoes which shoot out jets of liquid sulphur with more force than a missile shot from a fire-arm.

Saturn

From Earth, **Saturn** appears to be circled by thousands of rings. These rings are made up of hundreds of thousands of blocks of ice and rocks, the largest as large as a six-storey house. Saturn is made up mainly of helium and hydrogen at gaseous, liquid and solid state, and winds blow at a force of 1800 kilometres an hour.
Less dense than all the other planets, Saturn seems to be sunken in a great big ocean, making the planet appear yellow within it. The diameter of Saturn is 119,300 kilometres, the diameter of its rings at least 273,700 kilometres. On Saturn, one day lasts 10.2 Earth hours and one year equals 29.5 Earth years. The average distance from the Sun is estimated at 1427 million kilometres.

FACT

Of the 15 moons of **Uranus,** 10 were discovered only in 1986, thanks to the American Space Probe **Voyager 2.** The largest satellite, **Oberon**, has an impressive diameter of 1630 kilometres. And on the surface of the second largest moon, **Miranda,** there are craters ten times deeper than the Grand Canyon. The other moons each have a diameter of less than 80 kilometres.

Uranus

The axis of Uranus tilts back at 60°. This means that, within the space of one year on the planet, and which corresponds to 84 Earth years, both poles are illuminated constantly for 42 years, with a dark and constant night lasting the next 42 years. Uranus is four times larger than Earth, with 11 rings, just a few thousand metres thick and made up of millions of particle masses encircling its equator. The diameter of

Uranus is 51,800 kilometres and one day lasts 17.2 hours on Earth. The average distance from Uranus to the Sun is 2870 million kilometres.

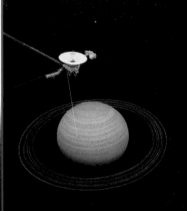

Right: Voyager 2 whilst in transit towards Uranus, 24 January 1986. Below, the surface of the planet.

The moons of Saturn

Saturn has the most moons – an astonishing 18! *Titan* is the second largest satellite in the Solar System, just a little smaller than *Ganymede,* one of the moons of Jupiter. One third of the surface of its satellite *Mimas* is covered by giant craters.

Neptune

Blanketed by thin clouds and encircled by a slender band of rings, **Neptune** boasts 8 moons. Its diameter is 49,500 kilometres, one day lasts 16.1 Earth hours, and one year on Neptune lasts 164.8 Earth years – far longer than the life of a human being. The average distance from Neptune to the Sun is 4497 kilometres.

Image of a Space Probe of a mission to explore the planets Neptune and Pluto within the next few years.

FACT

Pluto has just one giant moon – **Charon**, with a diameter of at least 1200 kilometres and its surface made up of ice as hard as rock.

26

Pluto

Pluto is the smallest planet and very cold (-280°C average temperature). It is the most distant in the Solar System. Its orbit is quite different to that of any of the other planets, slanting so much that, over a period of twenty years, this planet is sometimes to be found within the orbit of Neptune, as if on a 'heavenly roundabout'. Pluto's moon, **Charon,** is half as large as the planet itself, and it is the most distant satellite in the entire Solar System. The diameter of Pluto is 2300 kilometres and one day on the planet is equal to 6.4 days on Earth, with one year equal to 248 Earth years. The average distance from the Sun is 5915 kilometres. From the surface of Pluto, the Sun appears as a far distant and extremely bright star.

The Moons of Neptune

The largest of **Neptune's** 8 moons is **Triton** (shown in the illustration). Triton is the coldest place in all the Solar System -495°C. Despite the ice-covered surface, Triton shoots powerful jets of liquid oxygen into the face of the Universe, rather like a natural geyser on Earth. It is the only satellite which orbits its planet in the opposite direction to the movement of its rotation.

The Conquest of Space

4 October 1957	The Soviet Union launched the first artificial satellite, **Sputnik 1**. For the first time on 3 November of the same year, the Soviet Union sent a living thing – **a dog called Laika** – into space on board **Sputnik 2**.
31 January 1958	The USA launched their first artificial satellite, **Explorer 1**.
2 January 1958	Russian-built **Lunik 1** became the first artificial satellite to leave Earth's orbit and to pass over the Moon. On 12 September, **Lunik 2** became the first Space Probe to make a landing on the surface of the Moon. On 7 October of the same year, **Lunik 3** sent back the first photographic images of the 'hidden side' of the Moon.
1 April 1960	The USA launched the first weather satellite, **Tiros 1**.
12 April 1961	**Yuri A. Gagarin** on board the spacecraft **Vostok 1**, was the first man in space, orbiting around the Earth for 1 hour and 48 minutes.
20 February 1962	**John Glenn**, on board spacecraft **Mercury 6**, became the first American in orbit around the Earth. His space mission lasted about 5 hours.
6 July 1962	The USA launched the first telecommunications satellite, **Telstar 1**.

Sputnik 1

Spacecraft Mercury

Apollo 11. The Conquest of the Moon

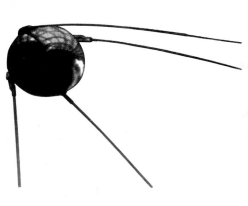

Space-Station *MIR*

3 October 1962	American astronaut **W. M. Schirra Jr.**, on board the spacecraft **Mercury 8**, established a record which is so far unbeaten. After completing 6 orbits around the Earth within a time of just over 8 hours, he then made a successful landing at 'just' 7 kilometres from the expected location.
16 June 1963	Russian **Valentina V. Tereskova**, on board **Vostok 6**, became the first woman in Space.
12 October 1964	Spacecraft **Voskhod 1** (USSR) was the first space vehicle with three cosmonauts on board.
18 March 1965	Soviet cosmonaut **A. Leonov**, on board the space mission **Voskhod 2**, completed the first 'walk' in space, leaving his spacecraft for ten minutes.
15 December 1965	USA spacecrafts *Gemini 6* and *Gemini 7* completed the first 'meeting' in orbit in the history of space flight.
24 December 1968	**Apollo 8**, with American astronauts **F. Borman**, **J. Lovell** and **W. Anders** on board, completed the first orbital flight around the Moon.

Voyager   *Space Shuttle*   *Galileo* Space Probe   *Hubble* Space Telescope

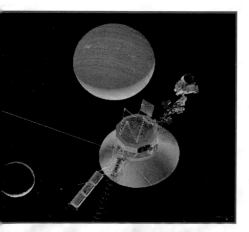

Index